E.L. Shuey

A Handbook of the United Brethren in Christ

E.L. Shuey

A Handbook of the United Brethren in Christ

ISBN/EAN: 9783743603233

Manufactured in Europe, USA, Canada, Australia, Japa

Cover: Foto ©Lupo / pixelio.de

Manufactured and distributed by brebook publishing software
(www.brebook.com)

E.L. Shuey

A Handbook of the United Brethren in Christ

A HAND-BOOK

OF THE

United Brethren in Christ.

E. L. SHUEY, A. M.,

Of Otterbein University.

DAYTON, OHIO:
UNITED BRETHREN PUBLISHING HOUSE.
1885.

Preface.

AN intelligent understanding of the character of the religious denomination to which he belongs is important to
every Christian. In a church like our own, in which the members so fully direct the policy and methods, all, even the
youngest, should be instructed in its history and work, its
principles and government. A full knowledge of our church's
history—its struggles, growth, and successes, its principles
and methods of work,—can not fail to enlist the enthusiasm
of its members, and to make them more devoted to its interests.

To the young people of the church that desire a knowledge
of its life, to those that have not access to more extended
books, to others that desire in a brief space an outline of the
work and history of the denomination, this little hand-book is
offered with the hope that, in part at least, it will meet their
wants. It is believed that such a compendium, brief enough
to be read in a short time, yet full enough to give the essential
facts, will be of daily service.

It is difficult in such small space to present more than a
slight outline. No attempt, therefore, has been made at extended research, the incidents of the history and the state-
ments of work and doctrine being collected from larger
sources.

From these causes and for these purposes, this hand-book
has been prepared, and is presented to the members of the
church.

3

Contents.

History and Doctrine.

"UNITED BRETHREN IN CHRIST," is the title of the church which, in the latter part of the last century, grew out of the religious awakening of William Otterbein and a number of his friends.

Philip William Otterbein, the leader of this movement, was a distinguished divine and missionary of the German Reformed Church, who was sent by the Synods of Holland, in 1752, from Dillenburg, Germany, to America. He was chosen for the mission because of his zeal and earnestness, and his deep devotion. As a young man he preached with great power and learning. It was not, however, till after his settlement at Lancaster, Pennsylvania, his first charge in America, that Otterbein, after much prayer, realized that God had poured upon him the spirit of grace and power. He now began to preach against the lifeless formality of the church, which had been thought sufficient by both ministry and people, and in the midst of which he had so long lived and worked. He therefore urged the necessity of a new birth and of experimental godliness.

7

While Mr. Otterbein was thus preaching, and establishing prayer-meetings, in which the laymen might have better opportunities for labor, Rev. Martin Boehm, a zealous Mennonite, having himself experienced a similar change of heart, was engaged in a different field in the same work. At a "great meeting," held about 1766,* in Isaac Long's barn, in Lancaster County, Pennsylvania, both these ministers, with many others, were present. At the close of a very earnest sermon by Mr. Boehm, Mr. Otterbein arose and embraced the preacher, crying, "We are brethren!" These words suggested, a number of years later, the name for the new denomination which finally sprung from this meeting.

From this time these brethren, with other ministers, all Germans, traveled extensively in Pennsylvania, Virginia, and Maryland, preaching to all that a vital union with Christ, in heart and life, is essential to religious growth. Otterbein himself was, in 1774, settled over a congregation at Baltimore, Maryland, which had withdrawn from the communion of the German Reformed Church. Here he remained until his death in 1813, directing and superintending the work begun in his young manhood.

It was not intended, at first, by these fellow-workers to organize a new church, but simply to awaken the people to the importance of conversion, or the new birth. While working with this

---

* See *Life of Otterbein*, by Prof. A. W. Drury, A. M., pages 117-122.

purpose, several years passed. Later it was decided to call a conference of the ministers devoted to the work to consider the best means of uniting and establishing the believers in the new life. This gathering was held in 1789, at Baltimore, when it was decided to continue the conferences as might seem best. Finally, in 1800, the societies interested in the movement united and formed the "United Brethren in Christ," with Mr. Otterbein and Mr. Boehm as bishops.

GROWTH.

From 1800 to 1815, the church grew slowly but steadily in the states already mentioned, its work being solely among the Germans. As many of its members emigrated to Ohio and the West, they carried forward the work, and in 1810 a new conference was formed west of the Alleghanies, known as the Miami. From this were formed, in 1818 and the years following, the Muskingum, Scioto, Indiana, and other conferences.

Among the men prominent in the movements of this and the succeeding period, besides Bishops Otterbein and Boehm, were Christian Newcomer, George Geeting, Andrew Zeller, Henry Spayth, and Henry Kumler, sr. The zeal and devotion of these and other earnest men were abundantly rewarded.

The first General Conference met, June 6th, 1815, near Mt. Pleasant, Pennsylvania, in a small log school-house. Fourteen ministers were present, from four states. After much prayer and deliberation, the Confession of Faith was adopted, together with a book of discipline, containing rules and directions for the government of the church.

About the same time a new period of growth began. The church, hitherto composed exclusively of Germans, began to find earnest supporters among the English settlers west of the Alleghanies, and these conferences gradually became English. The growth was now more rapid, for the field was wider. Ministers and people were zealous in spreading their belief farther and farther. As they emigrated north and west, new churches and new conferences were formed, and the succeeding decades showed marked growth. The church, which in 1820 had about one hundred and fourteen preachers, with thirty-six itinerants, and perhaps ten thousand members, included in 1845 five hundred and eighty-one preachers and about thirty-six thousand members.

In the earlier years John Russell, Joseph Hoffman, John McNamar, and others, and in the later years Wm. Davis, J. Griffith, W. R. Rhinehart, J. J. Glossbrenner, D. Edwards, and many others contributed to the establishment of the work of the church and of its principles. This was the period in which the position of the church was taken on many of the great moral questions which distinguish it; and the men of the time were worthy of the work.

The efforts of the church during these years were largely expended in the country districts, the

ministers for some reason avoiding the towns and
cities. Each itinerant had many appointments,
traveling from one to another, preaching at private houses, in barns, school-houses, or wherever
opportunity offered. His salary was small, often
but a few dollars, but he was always honored,
and the people everywhere received him with
kindness and hospitality.

The increasing growth of the church led to the
adoption, in 1841, of the Constitution, which has
since been the basis of the legislation of the various general conferences. This same growth had
led to the establishment, in 1834, of the *Religious
Telescope*, and the beginning of the printing house
of the church. It was but a little later, in 1845,
that the first steps in our educational history were
taken, and the first college was opened in 1847.
But progress was not yet stopped. Feeling that
the church is to carry the gospel to all the
earth, the Missionary Society was organized in
1853, and the first missionaries were appointed a
year later. In 1875 the women of the church
began their active, aggressive work in the Woman's Missionary Society. From the early cate-
chetical schools had come the Sunday-schools, first
organized about 1827. To supply their wants
were begun the *Children's Friend* and *Missionary
Visitor*, and later the various Bible lesson-helps,
now so important a part of our work.

During the later years, the church has been
occupied in the development of these various de-

partments of its work. Most of the men who
have been influential in these movements are
still living, earnest in their endeavors, and honored by their fellow-men. The growth continues,
the efforts to hold the early zeal and devotion are
unbroken, and the mission of the church — to
maintain decided positions on all questions of
Christian life — is daily fulfilled in the work of its
people. In 1884 there were thirteen hundred and
thirty-six itinerants, with one hundred and sixty-
six thousand three hundred and twenty-three
members, contributing almost a million of dollars
for church-work.

CONFESSION OF FAITH.
ADOPTED IN 1815.

In the name of God we declare and confess before all men, that we believe in the only true God,
the Father, the Son, and the Holy Ghost, that
these three are one: The Father in the Son, the
Son in the Father, and the Holy Ghost equal in
essence or being with both; that this triune God
created the heavens and the earth, and all that
in them is, visible as well as invisible, and further-
more sustains, governs, protects, and supports the
same.

We believe in Jesus Christ; that he is very God
and man; that he became incarnate by the power
of the Holy Ghost in the Virgin Mary, and was
born of her; that he is the Savior and Mediator
of the whole human race, if they with full faith

in him accept the grace proffered in Jesus; that this Jesus suffered and died on the cross for us, was buried, arose again on the third day, ascended into heaven, and sitteth on the right hand of God to intercede for us; and that he shall come again at the last day to judge the quick and the dead.

We believe in the Holy Ghost; that he is equal in being with the Father and the Son, and that he comforts the faithful, and guides them into all truth.

We believe in a Holy Christian Church, the communion of saints, the resurrection of the body, and life everlasting.

We believe that the Holy Bible, Old and New Testaments, is the word of God; that it contains the only true way to our salvation; that every true Christian is bound to acknowledge and receive it with the influence of the Spirit of God, as the only rule and guide; and that without faith in Jesus Christ, true repentance, forgiveness of sins, and following after Christ, no one can be a true Christian.

We also believe that what is contained in the Holy Scriptures, to-wit: The fall in Adam and redemption through Jesus Christ, shall be preached throughout the world.

We believe that the ordinances, viz: Baptism and the remembrance of the sufferings and death of our Lord Jesus Christ, are to be in use and practiced by all Christian societies; and that it is incumbent on all the children of God particularly

to practice them ; but the manner in which ought
always to be left to the judgment and understanding of every individual. ·Also the example of
washing feet is left to the judgment of every one,
to practice or not; but it is not becoming of any
of our preachers or brethren to traduce any of their
brethren whose judgment and understanding in
these respects is different from their own, either in
public or private. Whosoever shall make himself
guilty in this respect, shall be considered a tradu-
cer of his brethren, and shall be answerable for
the same.

POLITY.

The Church of the United Brethren in Christ is
not an off-shoot from any denomination, its founders having held in view the accomplishment of a
special mission. It did not arise from differences
in doctrine, for it presents no new doctrines of any
kind. Its beliefs are those of other evangelical
churches, and its theology is Arminian. It enjoins the ordinances presented by the Scriptures
and followed by the Christian churches in general.
Its founders united to emphasize the need of con-
secration of soul to God, and this has been its
spirit.

In its administration, it is distinguished as a
body in which the power is almost equally divided
between the ministry and the people. All officers
hold their place by consent of the members, ex-
pressed by vote either directly or by representa-

tives. The people choose the local church-officers, who form the majority of each official board; in many conferences, a lay delegate to the annual conference; and the delegates to each general conference. The annual conference chooses its presiding elders and other officers. The general conference elects all the officers and boards of the church.

But one order of ministers is recognized — that of *elders*. Bishops and presiding elders are chosen from among the elders simply as superintendents.

In supplying the congregations with ministers, the "itinerant system" is the adopted method. All pastors are subject to settlement and change as determined by the committee chosen by each annual conference. A minister may not remain upon a charge more than three years without consent of two-thirds of the annual conference.

In form of worship the church seeks directness and simplicity. She has no liturgy and does not enforce uniformity in service, each congregation deciding the method for itself.

The meetings of the church include the regular Sabbath preaching of God's word, the weekly prayer and class-meetings, and the Sunday-school, with such others as each congregation may determine. Four times during the year the "quarterly meeting" of each charge is held by the presiding elder, at which time the general business of the charge is transacted, the communion service usually being held upon the Sabbath.

POSITION ON MORAL LIFE.

A natural result of the principles which led to
the formation of the church has been to require of
its members devotion to Christ, simplicity of faith,
purity of life, and uprightness of conduct. Upon
all questions of morality the position of the church
has always been decided. No compromise with
evil has been suggested.

The law of the church forbids the sale or use
of intoxicating liquors by its members; and the
renting of property to liquor dealers, or signing a
petition favoring them, is considered immoral. The
members are always found active in every movement for the growth of temperance. Against the
use of tobacco the sentiment is strong. Many
conferences refuse to admit to the ministry those
who use it in any way.

Slavery was always thought to be a sin, and in
1821 was entirely forbidden, the holding of slaves
being made a misdemeanor. This position has
never been changed. Many members in former
days suffered severely in defense of this principle.

The church has always held that secret societies
are evil in their nature and tendency; that union
with them is inconsistent with Christian life. Its
laws, therefore, forbid its members to hold connection with such societies, and provide stringent
rules for the violation of these provisions.

The authority of the civil government is recognized, and the members are enjoined to obey its
laws; and while disapproving warfare, the church

acknowledges the obligation of every citizen to protect and preserve the government in time of treason and invasion.

On the questions of the observance of the Sabbath, of divorce, of the true rights of man, the position of the church is undoubted. Its principles and its practice can not fail to lead to high Christian life.

2

Government.

ADOPTED IN 1841.

We, the members of the CHURCH OF THE UNITED BRETHREN IN CHRIST, in the name of God, do, for the perfecting of the saints, for the work of the ministry, for the edifying of the body of Christ, as well as to produce and secure a uniform mode of action, in faith and practice, also to define the powers and the business of quarterly, annual, and general conferences, as recognized by this church, ordain the following articles of CONSTITUTION:

ARTICLE I.

SECTION I. All ecclesiastical power herein granted, to make or repeal any rule of Discipline, is vested in a General Conference, which shall consist of elders, elected by the members in every conference district throughout the society; provided, however, such elders shall have stood in that capacity three years, in the conference district to which they belong.

SEC. 2. General Conference is to be held every four years; the bishops to be considered members and presiding officers.

SEC. 3. Each annual conference shall place before the society the names of all the elders eligible to membership in the General Conference.

18

ARTICLE II.

SECTION 1. The General Conference shall define the boundaries of the annual conferences.

SEC. 2. The General Conference shall, at every session, elect bishops from among the elders throughout the church, who have stood six years in that capacity.

SEC. 3. The business of each annual conference shall be done strictly according to Discipline; and any annual conference acting contrary thereunto, shall, by impeachment, be tried by the General Conference.

SEC. 4. No rule or ordinance shall at any time be passed, to change or do away the Confession of Faith as it now stands, nor to destroy the itinerant plan.

SEC. 5. There shall no rule be adopted that will infringe upon the rights of any as it relates to the mode of baptism, the sacrament of the Lord's-supper, or the washing of feet.

SEC. 6. There shall be no rule made that will deprive local preachers of their votes in the annual conferences to which they severally belong.

SEC. 7. There shall be no connection with secret combinations, nor shall involuntary servitude be tolerated in any way.

SEC. 8. The right of appeal shall be inviolate.

ARTICLE III.

The right, title, interest, and claim of all property, whether consisting in lots of ground, meeting-

houses, legacies, bequests or donations of any kind,
obtained by purchase or otherwise, by any person
or persons, for the use, benefit, and behoof of the
Church of the United Brethren in Christ, is hereby
fully recognized and held to be the property of the
church aforesaid.

ARTICLE IV.

There shall be no alteration of the foregoing
constitution, unless by request of two thirds of
the whole society.

OUTLINE OF THE CHURCH-GOVERNMENT.

An outline of the government of the church
must include a statement of its membership and
its division into conferences, of the ministry and
its character, and of the officers and official boards.

The basis of organization is the class, or congregation. For the sake of strength, several of these
classes may be united, forming a charge or circuit.
These stations and circuits are united into confer-
ence-districts, of which there are now about fifty.
These annual conferences are grouped at present
into five districts, each presided over by a bishop.

I. MEMBERSHIP. — The membership of the
church consists of those who have been formally
received in open congregation by the pastor, opportunity having been given for objections to their
reception. Before they are received, applicants
must affirm their belief in the Bible as the word
of God and the only guide to the knowledge of
the way of salvation; their confidence in the par-

don of their sins; their determination by the grace of God to follow Christ in a life of holiness and devotion; their willingness to be governed by the church-discipline.

Persons who are sincerely seeking the Lord may be received into the watch-care of the church, but are not reported as members, nor do they have a vote in the elections.

It is the duty of every member to acknowledge his faith in the Bible and its teachings; observe all the ordinances of God's house; attend the meetings of the church; encourage the Sunday-school; keep the Sabbath holy; be diligent in prayer; live a quiet and peaceable life among his fellows; pay liberally to the support of the ministry and of the church; and contribute freely to the benevolent work of God's people.

Persons guilty of misdemeanors or violations of church-rules, may, after due admonition and form of examination, be expelled by a vote of the class.

Members removing from any place may receive, by a vote of the charge, a certificate signed by the pastor recommending them to Christian fellowship elsewhere.

II. MINISTRY. — In close and natural relation to the membership, and springing from it, is the ministry, which is either itinerant or local. The former is the body of active preachers in charge of the various stations. The latter consists of those who, on account of sickness or other causes, have left the active work for a season.

In the choice of the ministry, the official members exercise the authority of the church.

Each quarterly conference is authorized to issue a license to any person, properly qualified, as exhorter. This must be renewed annually. Such persons may then publicly explain the Scriptures.

Any person desiring to enter the ministry must apply to the quarterly conference of the church of which he is a member. He must give satisfactory evidence of his conversion, of his knowledge and qualifications, of his call to the ministry, and of his willingness to obey the church-laws. His license is renewable annually, and he must pursue the course of reading prescribed by the Discipline of the church. After holding this relation one or more years, the licentiate may be recommended to the annual conference for admission as a preacher. He must here be examined upon his faith, experience, desires, determinations, and qualifications. If these be satisfactory he may be admitted as a preacher, upon probation. During the three years of this probation, the young minister must pursue the course of reading prescribed by the church, being examined each year upon the studies of that year. At the close of this probation, after a full examination of his character and attainments, the applicant may be admitted to the order of *elder*. The ordination service, usually performed by the bishop, by the laying on of hands, is conducted on a day appointed,—generally at the meeting of the annual conference.

Having been thus admitted to the conference, the elder accepts the duties of the itinerant, is eligible to a minister's privileges, and is permitted to perform all the offices ordinarily belonging to him.

The minister, or elder, not only is the spiritual leader and instructor of the church, but keeps its records of members, arranges for the collection of the contributions to the benevolences of the church, and superintends all its work.

The support of the ministry is provided by the people. At the beginning of each year the salary, as agreed upon by the minister and people, is apportioned among the members, and it is collected during the year by the proper officers. In cases where needed, assistance is given from the funds of the Board of Missions, either of the church or of the conference. Provision is also made for the support of worn-out itinerant ministers and their families by general contributions of the people, and by payments from surplus funds of the Print- ing Establishment.

III. OFFICERS.—The *local officers* of each church are the class leaders, class stewards, and trustees. The members of each church are divided into as many classes as is thought desirable. Each class then chooses its leader and steward. However, if the class prefer it, the pastor may appoint the *steward*.

The *Class Leader* is to be the spiritual guide of his class. Being a faithful student of the Scriptures, a pious and godly man, he is to be an example to all his circle. It is his duty to meet his class in prayer and conference meetings, to speak to them regarding their Christian life, to visit them when sick, and to encourage them when in difficulty.

The *Class Steward* collects the contributions for the support of the ministry and church, keeps an accurate account of all money received, and reports the same to the treasurer at the quarterly conference. In congregations in which payments for church-expenses are made by envelopes deposited at the church each Sabbath, the stewards serve as efficient assistants to the treasurer.

The expenses of the church are met by subscriptions made at the beginning of the conference year, or by assessments upon the members made by the finance committee on an estimate of the annual expenditure. These estimates may include whatever items are desired by the church.

The *Trustees* are the legal representatives of the church. They are chosen by the quarterly conference in accordance with the law of the state. They have charge of all church property, controlling the building of churches and parsonages, and having direct care of them. They are authorized to receive and make deeds for property.

The *Official Board* of each congregation transacts the general business. It is composed of the pastor, all properly recognized preachers, exhorters, leaders, stewards, trustees of property, and superintendents of Sunday-schools, that reside within the bounds of the congregation. This board, meeting monthly, chooses the secretary and treasurer of the church, appoints and receives reports of committees, and transacts all the business of the congregation. It submits the record of its business to the quarterly conference.

The ministerial and executive officers are the presiding elders and bishops. These are always ministers, and are chosen by the elders at the annual and general conferences.

The *Presiding Elders* are chosen by the annual conference from among its body of elders. The conference having been divided into districts, an officer is placed over each. These presiding elders hold the quarterly meetings at each station, inquire into the condition of the work, spiritual and temporal, and assist the pastors in every way possible. The salary of each is fixed by the annual conference, and is assessed upon the various charges of the district.

The *Bishops* are chosen from among the elders, by the general conference, at each of its sessions. These are the superintendents of the church, each presiding over a district, of which there are (1884) five. They preside at the annual and general conferences, and attend to the execution of the laws of the church. They hold annual meetings for deciding questions of law, determining the time of holding the annual conferences, and considering the general interests of the church.

They spend much time in visiting the various conferences, consulting, dedicating churches, and assisting the ministers. Their salaries are fixed by the general conference, and are apportioned among the various conferences of each district, to be paid by the subscriptions of the people.

IV. CONFERENCES.—Closely related to the official meeting, and composed of the same members, is the *Quarterly Conference.* This meets four times each year, as appointed by the presiding elder, who presides over its sessions. This body makes the settlements with the stewards and ministers; grants licenses to exhort or preach; inquires into the moral and official character of its members; makes estimates of the expenses of the station or circuit, and provides for their apportionment.

Beyond the congregation and the circuit is the *Annual Conference.* This consists of all elders and licentiate preachers that have been duly received by the conference. In addition each conference has the right to provide for the election of one layman from each charge. This has been done by many conferences, thus giving the laymen active participation in the control of the church and in consultation for its interests.

This conference has general supervision of the work within its limits; fixes the boundaries of stations and circuits; considers the religious work of the church—missions, Sunday-schools, etc.; receives reports from the ministers, including the money raised for general church purposes, and ex-

amines the moral and official character of each minister; provides for the examination and ordination
of candidates for the ministry; hears appeals from
the congregations; chooses presiding elders and
other officers; and appoints committees which,
with the bishop, station the presiding elders and
ministers.

The meeting of the annual conference is always
an incident of great interest and blessing to the
people, and is one of the church's most efficient
means of union and Christian fellowship.

The important bond of union for the church in
general is the *General Conference*, which meets every
four years on the second Thursday in May, at such
place as may be designated. This conference consists of ministers chosen by the vote of the members of the denomination during the month of
November preceding its session. Each annual
conference is entitled to not less than two nor
more than four representatives, according to the
number of its members.

The general conference examines the administration of each annual conference, and establishes
its boundaries; prescribes the districts and assigns
to each bishop his work; modifies the provisions
of the church Discipline; provides for the management of the various institutions of church-work;
and elects the general officers,—bishops, publishing
agent, editors of periodicals, secretary and treasurer of the Missionary Society, trustees of the
Seminary and Publishing House, and members of

the educational, missionary, and Sunday-school
boards.

Thus the general conference gives direction to
the thought and power of the church, and be-
comes the exponent of its faith and spirit. Its
influence in the church, in uniting its interests
and directing its energies, and in bringing together
its people and teaching them the blessings of
Christian fellowship, can not be over-estimated.

Departments of Church-Work.

The church, realizing that the efforts of its members must be exerted in specific directions; that God has commanded his people to study his word, to instruct others, and to preach his gospel; and that system is essential to the best results of labor, has recognized various departments for the exertion of its energies. These include the Sunday-school, the missionary, the publishing, and the educational interests.

These institutions have earned, by their blessed results, the enthusiastic support of every one, and may well call forth the honest pride of all members.

I. SUNDAY-SCHOOLS.

From its beginning provision has been made by the church for the instruction of the youth in the way of the Lord. Sunday-schools for instruction in the catechism were held very early. Otterbein himself visited parts of the church and "started prayer-meetings and Sunday-schools" very early in the century. The first school in Baltimore was begun in 1827, at the old Otterbein Church. From that time every encouragement has been given to instruction in the word of God.

The Sunday-school has ever been considered a department of the church, working in and with

29

the church.   The superintendent is a church
officer, responsible to the quarterly conference.
On the other hand, the church is charged with
nourishing and encouraging the school.

For the promotion of the interests of this cause
a Sunday-school Board is appointed by each general
conference.   The board employs a secretary, who
holds institutes for instruction in Sunday-school
work, assists in the organization and direction of
new or weak schools, and gives aid and counsel
wherever needed.   The board also, through its
treasurer, disburses the money of the Sunday-
school fund, which is paid in by the schools and
congregations.   This fund is used to assist weak
schools in new localities, furnishing supplies as
they may be needed.   This is one of the most
worthy of the church-benevolences, the small
amount expended doing vast good.   In addition,
this board plans and suggests methods for the
improvement and enlargement of the Sunday-
school work and influence.   Upon its suggestion,
in order that the children may be more specific-
ally instructed in the history and interests of the
church, the first Sunday in June, being that nearest
Otterbein's birthday, is fixed as *Children's Day*.
The services of this day are all for children, while
the contributions go to augment the board's permanent fund.   There is also provided a course of
study for the preparation of Sunday-school teachers.   Diplomas are given, signed by the president
and secretary, to all who complete this "Normal

Course." A "Reading Circle" has been formed, under the direction of the board, for the promotion of culture in the church.

As a result of energy in this department of the church - work, the Sunday - schools are unusually prosperous. In 1884 there were 3,228 schools, with 167,645 scholars, and 27,377 officers and teachers, being 28,699 more than the total membership of the church. From these schools has come much of the strength of the church, and many of its best workers are trained in them. For a number of years Col. Robert Cowden has been the efficient secretary of the board, and much of the growth is due to his energy.

II. MISSIONS.

The various conferences have been interested during most of the church's history, in the spread of the Gospel beyond their immediate limits, and many have supported missionaries in home fields. Indeed, the history of the church has been that of mission-work, and the denomination is essentially missionary.

There was, however, during the earlier years, no union of effort for foreign missions. The first suggestions in their favor were decidedly opposed by many. The general conferences of 1841, 1845, and 1849, took some inefficient action upon the subject. During these years, as a result of agitation, opinions were changing and the sentiment in favor of foreign work was growing. Some of the annual conferences were very earnest, and began to move toward active effort. Finally, in 1853, the general conference organized the "HOME, FRONTIER, AND FOREIGN MISSIONARY SOCIETY," and appointed a board of directors and the proper officers. Rev. J. C. Bright, of the Sandusky Conference, through whose efforts, especially, these results were reached, was the first secretary.

The newly appointed board met at Westerville, Ohio, in June, 1854. After much deliberation it was decided to send a missionary to West Africa. Rev. W. J. Shuey, who had constantly urged the action, was then appointed the first missionary. As his companions, Dr. D. C. Kumler, and Rev. D. K. Flickinger, were chosen. These sailed from New York in January, 1855, reaching Freetown a month later. After much difficulty a deed was obtained for the present mission-station at Shaingay, in British Sherbro, sixty miles south of Freetown, Sierra Leone.

The history of this mission from that time till 1870, is an index of the mission-spirit of the people of America. It is a history of struggle, discouragement, and indifference even, at home, and of difficulty and opposition abroad. Among those who gave their services and labored faithfully were Rev. D. K. Flickinger, D. D., whose devotion to our missions has been of great importance; Rev. J. K. Billheimer and wife, so closely identified with the church's missionary efforts; Rev. W. B. Witt; Rev. C. O. Wilson ; Rev. O. Hadley and wife ; and

Rev. J. A. Williams, a native Christian, who gave efficient service, being often the only one in charge.

In 1869 a crisis was reached, and the abandonment of the work was seriously considered. But, largely through the influence of Rev. J. Kemp, better counsels prevailed and a new effort was made. Mr. and Mrs. J. Gomer, members of the colored church at Dayton, Ohio, were sent out to begin anew the work among the heathen. From that time the work has steadily grown and its influence widened. Now there are twelve missionaries, with twenty-four native assistants, fifteen stations, two hundred and fifty-six towns reached, and four hundred and forty-four members. The property at the various points is of great value.

In 1883 the American Missionary Association transferred to the board for a term of years the Mendi-Mission, near Shaingay, with its annual income of $5,000. With this came funds for building a small steamer for use at the missions. Christians in England about the same time became interested in the success of our missions, and have promised material aid.

The methods of work employed commend themselves to all. In addition to the religious teaching, boys and girls are received into the schools and taught much as Americans are taught, the instruction including various trades and industries. The mission farm is carefully tilled, and its products bring a good income. Thus careful habits, love of

c

work, and a knowledge of the arts of civilization, are given with the religious instruction. Several natives—D. F. Wilberforce, David Kasambo, and Remmie Caulker — have been brought to America and educated as a preparation for the work in their own land.

Western Africa seems to be the peculiar field of the church, and increasing success attends its efforts.

The board has carried its foreign work also into Germany, for the propagation of evangelical religion in that land. This work was begun in 1869, Rev. C. Bischoff being the first missionary. The work has grown until about sixty towns in Germany are reached by our workers, of whom there are twelve. These churches have over six hundred members. The ministers preach the same doctrine as did Otterbein, in the century before,— the need of conversion, and a life devoted to God's service.

Nor is the work of the Missionary Society confined to foreign fields. From its inception a large part of its work has been the extension of the church into new fields, especially on the frontier. The missionaries sent out have followed the line of emigration in the West and Northwest, enduring untold hardships for the sake of the work. Of the stations thus established the board assumes control, forming mission districts and mission conferences, providing many of the ministers and much of their support. The growth of the church in the West has been due largely to these efforts. The home fields — those within the bounds of the annual conferences — are under the direction of the conferences themselves, as branches of the general society.

In 1884 there were reported, in home and frontier fields, 397 missionaries, preaching at 1,357 places. There was collected for missions, in the same period, $47,404.16.

As stated before, the Missionary Society is simply the church organized for mission-work. The management is entrusted to a Board of Directors chosen by the general conference, and consisting of a president, four vice-presidents, secretary, treasurer, and seven directors. The payment of ten dollars at one time constitutes a life member of the society, and of fifty dollars, a life director. These members may serve on committees and discuss questions at the annual meetings of the board, but have no right to vote.

The board holds its meetings at such time and place as it may itself determine. It opens missions; employs missionaries; directs the various mission districts and conferences; makes appropriations for the different parts of its work; and consults and legislates generally for the cause of missions throughout the church. It appoints an executive committee to direct the work between its sessions.

The secretary and treasurer devote their time exclusively to the interests of the society,—keeping its records, visiting its missions, attending conferences, soliciting funds, and instructing and encouraging the church in the work.

Each conference is a branch society, controlling the missions in its own territory. It pays a fixed proportion of its receipts into the treasury of the general board, which largely depends upon it for support. The conferences usually assess a definite amount upon each charge within their limits, this amount being then paid by the members during the church-year.

The CHURCH-ERECTION SOCIETY is under the control of the Missionary Society, and is managed by its officers. This branch of the work has as its object the loaning of money to needy societies for the building of churches. When help is needed, application is made to the Board of Directors, the money is loaned on security, and is returned without interest within three years. The money is largely raised, as are the missionary funds, by the contributions of the membership upon assessment by the conferences. This feature of the church-work is worthy of greater support than it has ever received.

The WOMAN'S MISSIONARY SOCIETY was organized in 1875, at Dayton, Ohio, eight conferences being represented. Without hesitation the work was begun by the appointment of Miss Emily Beeken as missionary to Africa. A station, known as Rotofunk, was chosen, near enough to Shaingay to co-operate with the missionaries of the general board, yet far enough to open a new country to Christianity.

In 1877, Mrs. M. M. Mair, of Scotland, relieved Miss Beeken. By energy and devotion the work grew, new stations were opened and schools begun, and the whole was now called Bompeh Mission. In 1882 Mr. and Mrs. R. N. West relieved Mrs. Mair, who returned home for rest. In 1884, five mission-aries and teachers were employed, reaching 38 towns; and the members numbered 131. This board owns a good mission-house and chapel, cost-ing about $5,000, with fine grounds.

With the growth of the work, the power to act was increased; and, in 1880, a mission was begun in Coburg, Germany. This has grown in numbers and influence. In 1882, in response to repeated calls, it was decided to open work among the Chinese of the Pacific coast. A year later Rev. and Mrs. George A. Sickafoose were appointed to the work at Portland, Oregon. Here they have an attendance at the school of about sixty, and have organized a church with twenty-eight members.

The *Woman's Evangel*, a monthly paper estab-lished in 1881, and published at Dayton, Ohio, is the organ of the association.

In 1884, the sum of $6,654.24 was collected.

This society has taken especial charge of the in-struction of the children and youth of the church in the work of missions, and many of these are learning to love and encourage not only the mis-sion-work, but all the work of the church.

Each step taken in our mission-history has shown the blessing of God,—the interest has increased, the contributions have grown, and men and women in many parts of the world have received the gospel. The purpose of organization is daily fulfilled.

III. THE PRINTING ESTABLISHMENT.

In 1829, Aaron Farmer, of Salem, Indiana, began, under the auspices of the Miami Conference, the publication of the *Zion's Advocate*, a small religious paper. This was the first attempt at a church paper. The enterprise soon failed from want of patronage, but it served to awaken an interest in church-literature. The general conference of 1833 resolved to establish a religious paper, and appointed three trustees, who were authorized to collect subscriptions and donations, and to publish a "paper devoted to religious, moral, and literary intelligence." The next year these trustees bought property, presses, and materials at Circleville, Ohio, valued at $1,600. The *Mountain Messenger*, of Hagerstown, Maryland, undertaken a few months before, was purchased a little later, and its editor, Rev. W. R. Rhinehart, was made editor of the new enterprise. The first number of *The Religious Telescope*, a small semi-monthly, was issued, December 31, 1834. This was the beginning of the publishing interest of the church, which has now grown to be one of its greatest and most important factors of usefulness.

The one paper then published had a circulation of about one thousand, which at one time fell to

a little more than half that number, and most of
this was unpaid.   It was but a short time, therefore, till there was a growing debt.   But good management relieved this before 1849.   During these
years Revs. N. Altman and W. Hanby were
employed as agents.   In 1853, the general conference decided to remove the Printing Establishment
to Dayton, Ohio, and accordingly the trustees
purchased the site now held, one of the best in
the city, for about $11,000.00.   Rev. S. Vonneida
was agent at that time, and Rev. H. Kumler, jr.,
assistant.   The credit system was in vogue, and the
failure to pay the bills due almost overwhelmed
the business.   In 1864, a debt of $52,000 had been
created, while the assets were invoiced at about
$63,000.   At this time Mr. T. N. Sowers was chosen
agent, and soon after Rev. W. J. Shuey succeeded
him.   The agent then proposed as a method of re-
lief the "Publication Fund," to be contributed
by the church.   This plan, adopted by the general
conference of 1865, brought $19,000 to the estab-
lishment, and gave it an impetus in the right direction.   Though the struggle was long, yet by
careful management and judicious use of resources,
the agent was able to pay the last of the debt in
1880.   Since then the assets have increased to
over $200,000, the business has been greatly en-
larged, and its credit firmly established.

The establishment includes all the departments
necessary for complete work—wholesale and retail
book-rooms; press, job-printing, news, and mail-

ing-rooms; bindery; electrotype and stereotype foundry, and editorial departments. It employs a large number of men and women, and does a business of several hundred thousand dollars a year.

Besides the many books prepared for the church, numerous periodicals are published. The oldest of these, *The Religious Telescope*, begun under such unfavorable circumstances, has grown to be a strong and influential weekly. Among its editors have been some of the most prominent men of the church. A list of their names may be found in the Historical Tables, on page 47. The Sunday-school literature, long edited by Dr. D. Berger, includes the *Children's Friend, Our Bible Teacher*, the *Lesson Quarterlies*, and *For the Little Ones*. The *Missionary Visitor* is edited by the secretary of the Missionary Society. The circulation of these papers is not confined to our own church, but their excellence has carried them far beyond its limits. The German papers, *Der Froeliche Botschafter* and *Jugend Pilger*, edited for many years by Rev. W. Mittendorf, though they have a more restricted circulation, reach the homes and schools of the German portion of the church.

The establishment is controlled by a Board of Trustees, elected every four years by the general conference. Under this board is the publishing agent, chosen also by the general conference. These are the business managers of the house, fixing salaries of its general officers, controlling its property, and planning for the extension of the work. The agent has immediate charge of all the business, appoints and pays all subordinates, manages all its commercial enterprises, and is responsible for all its work. Besides these business officers are the editor of the *Religious Telescope* and his assistant, the editor of the Sunday-school literature and his assistant, and the editor of the German papers, who direct the various periodicals with which they are connected.

The Discipline provides that the profits of the establishment, beyond what are necessary as a reserve, shall be distributed among the conferences, according to the number of itinerants, for the benefit of worn-out preachers and their families. Such a distribution has been made in recent years from the funds accumulated through the excellent management of the resources of the establishment.

IV. EDUCATIONAL WORK.

The energy of the church was so fully occupied, during its early history, with the work of evangelization that but little thought was given to educational questions. The members were largely Germans to whom an educated ministry was synonymous with formality and skepticism. The members generally were intelligent people and believers in the public schools, and many of the ministers were well educated. Bishop Otterbein was one of the most learned men of his time. But none of these thought of education as a part of the church's work.

Finally, in 1845, the general conference recommended to the conferences a consideration of the question of the establishment of a church-college. In accord with the custom of the time, each conference began to agitate the question of an institution for itself, instead of one central university for the church. The Scioto Conference was the first to turn its discussions into action. In 1846, it purchased, for about $1,300, "Blendon Young Men's Seminary," at Westerville, Ohio. This was soon after incorporated as "Otterbein University of Ohio," and was opened for students in 1847, — the first church institution of learning. Other conferences soon joined the Scioto in the project and united almost all of Ohio. President Lewis Davis, D. D., so long connected with Otterbein University, and later with Union Biblical Seminary, was foremost among the men to whom belongs the honor of pressing forward the educational work of the church in this period of decided and continued opposition.

This was the beginning of what may be termed the formative period of our educational history, which has been᾿ marked by the organization of very many institutions,—some of them successful, others partially or wholly failing.

Mt. Pleasant Institute, of Pennsylvania, was founded by the Alleghany Conference three years after Otterbein University, and after an existence of over ten years was united with it. Five years after the opening of Otterbein University,

Hartsville College was founded by the conferences of southern Indiana. Later, in 1856, Western College, now at Toledo, Iowa, was begun at Western, Iowa, for the church west of the Mississippi. A number of years afterward, Lebanon Valley College was established in the East, and Westfield College, in Illinois. After these institutions, others were founded in various parts of the church, as occasion seemed to demand. Many of these are academies, and serve as preparatory to the higher work of the colleges.

These colleges and academies have all done good work, and most of them are growing slowly in attendance and resources. None of them has been able, however, from lack of extended support, to attain the university rank so much desired.

UNION BIBLICAL SEMINARY, the theological school of the denomination, is the result of an imperative demand on the part of the entire church. As the colleges grew in influence, and became centers of religious power instead of promoters of formality and skepticism, as had been predicted in early times, the need of an institution for the special preparation of the ministry was demonstrated. After full deliberation, Union Biblical Seminary was established at Dayton, Ohio, by order of the general conference of 1869. Dr. L. Davis was called from Otterbein University to be its senior professor, Revs. G. A. Funkhouser, D. D., and J. P. Landis, D. D., being chosen as associates. For a number of years the Summit Street United

Brethren Church was used for the work of the school, but in 1879 a building was erected in West Dayton. The seminary has proved itself, in these few years, a most valuable influence in our church-history. It is in pressing need, however, of more money, and the church should feel more fully its importance as a factor in its life.

THE BOARD OF EDUCATION, of twelve members, is elected by each general conference. The objects of this board are to awaken the church to a fuller appreciation of the value of an educated membership and ministry ; to collect funds for the assistance of young persons who are preparing for the ministry ; to recommend to the colleges and academies such measures as will make them more efficient ; to collect statistics of the institutions of the church and report them to the general conference.

In accordance with these provisions, the board has suggested that the church join in the observance of the "Day of Prayer for Colleges"—the last Thursday of January ; that on the following Sabbath collections be taken in all the congregations for the "Beneficiary Fund." This fund is loaned to young men, without interest, to assist them in their preparation for the work of the ministry.

The board meets annually at the Seminary at Dayton, during the first week of May. It has had a good influence in bringing together many of those most interested in education, and in suggesting plans for growth.

Conclusion.

A study of the faith, polity, and work of our church, even brief as the foregoing, may be found very suggestive. It has been seen that in belief the church teaches a pure faith in salvation through the atonement of Christ; that in government it is as liberal as is consistent with efficiency; that in worship its forms are simple and unadorned; that in life it enjoins the highest godliness. The history shows that the church has grown slowly but steadily, through the devotion of earnest workers, many of whom have sacrificed much for its life; that little by little its field has been widened, first in the extension of its territory, afterwards in the development of its departments of effort; that these departments, while they have grown in extent and influence, have been retarded by the lack of adequate moral and financial support.

This same study presents, also, some of the existing needs. If the purpose of the church is to be fulfilled, earnest labor for its extension, devotion to the work of Christ, and purity of life and thought, are required. Its beliefs and polity settled, the development of its various departments of work must be pushed forward with

energy. Our missionary and educational interests — the parts most dependent upon the benev-
olence of the members — need more earnest and
enthusiastic support. Each member must realize
that he is responsible for a portion of the work of
the church in the spreading of the Gospel, both
for the salvation of the heathen in distant lands
and for the extension of the church in our own
land. Parents must feel the importance of
thorough education, in our own schools, for
their children, if the church is to have such a
membership as may be able to present its claims
in an educated world. Young people must grow
to a deeper desire for the knowledge which our
schools and colleges can supply. In our church-
publications are the elements of intelligence, union,
and strength ; hence, these should receive constant
support, both in the purchase of books and periodicals and in the enlargement of the circle of pa-
trons. Old and young should feel that these are
church-interests, designed to promote the growth
and to assist the work of its members, upon whom
is the responsibility of success.

Our church has won for itself a worthy place
among Christian denominations. It has done
much for the salvation of men. But its influence
will be widened only as its members are devoted
to its work and its interests. To secure the great-
est results in earnest Christian labor, a broad and
enthusiastic church-spirit must be cultivated.

HISTORICAL TABLES.

GENERAL OFFICERS.

BISHOPS.

1800—1813, William Otterbein (died, 1813) and Martin Boehm (died, 1812).

1813—1814, Christian Newcomer.

1814—1815, Christian Newcomer.

1815—1817, Christian Newcomer and Andrew Zeller.

1817—1821, Christian Newcomer and Andrew Zeller.

1821—1825, Christian Newcomer and Joseph Hoffman.

1825—1829, Christian Newcomer and Henry Kumler, sen.

1829—1833, Christian Newcomer (died in 1830), and Henry Kumler, sen.

1833—1837, Henry Kumler, sen., Samuel Hiestand, and William Brown.

1837—1841, Henry Kumler, sen., Samuel Hiestand (died, 1838), and Jacob Erb.

1841—1845, Henry Kumler, sen., Jacob Erb, Henry Kumler, jun., and John Coons.

1845—1849, John Russel, J. J. Glossbrenner, and William Hanby.

1849—1853, J. J. Glossbrenner, Jacob Erb, and David Edwards.

1853—1857, J. J. Glossbrenner, David Edwards, and Lewis Davis.

1857—1861, J. J. Glossbrenner, David Edwards. Lewis Davis, D. D., and John Russel.

1861—1865, J. J. Glossbrenner, David Edwards, Jacob Markwood, Daniel Shuck, and Henry Kumler, jun.

1865—1869, J. J. Glossbrenner, David Edwards, Jacob Markwood, Jonathan Weaver, and Daniel Shuck.

1869—1873, J. J. Glossbrenner, David Edwards, D. D., Jonathan Weaver, and John Dickson.

1873—1877, J. J. Glossbrenner, David Edwards, D. D., (died, 1876), Jonathan Weaver, D. D., and John Dickson.

1877—1881, J. J. Glossbrenner, Jonathan Weaver, D. D., John Dickson, D. D., Milton Wright, D. D., and Nicholas Castle.

1881—1885, J. J. Glossbrenner, D. D., Jonathan Weaver, D. D., John Dickson, D. D., E. B. Kephart, D. D., and Nicholas Castle.

AGENTS OF THE PRINTING ESTABLISHMENT.

Three Trustees—John Russel, John Dresbach,
    George Dresbach ....1834 to 1839.
Rev. Wm. Hanby, Agent and Editor.....................1839 to 1845.
Rev. J. Markwood (elected, but did not serve).......1845
Rev. N. Altman................................... ....1845 to 1852.
Rev. Wm. Hanby...................................1852 to 1853.
Rev. S. Vonneida.....................................1853 to 1861.
    Assistants : Rev. H. Kumler, jun...................1854
                  T. N. Sowers...............................1854 to 1861.
T. N. Sowers and J. B. King............................1861 to 1864.
T. N. Sowers and Rev. W. J. Shuey....................1864 to 1865.
Rev. W. J. Shuey and T. N. Sowers.....................1865
Rev. W. J. Shuey and Rev. Wm. McKee...............1865 to 1866.
Rev. W. J. Shuey.......................................1866............

EDITORS OF THE "RELIGIOUS TELESCOPE."

Rev. Wm. Rhinehart...................................1834 to 1839.
Rev. Wm. Hanby......................................1839 to 1845.
Rev. D. Edwards............... ....1845 to 1849.
Rev. Wm. Hanby...... ....1849 to 1852.
    Assistant : Rev. John Lawrence....................1850 to 1852.
Rev. John Lawrence...................................1852 to 1864.
Rev. D. Berger.......................................1864 to 1869.
Rev. M. Wright.......................................1869 to 1873.
Rev. M. Wright and Rev. W. O. Tobey, A. M.........1873 to 1877.
Rev. J. W. Hott, D. D....................................1877............
    Assistants : Rev. W. O. Tobey, A. M.............1877 to 1881.
                Rev. M. R. Drury, A. M...............1881............

EDITORS OF SABBATH-SCHOOL PERIODICALS.

Rev. D. Edwards ....1854 to 1857.
Rev. S. Vonneida...1857 to 1869.
Rev. D. Berger, D. D...............................1869.............

EDITORS OF GERMAN PAPERS.

Rev. Jacob Erb...1841 to 1842.
Rev. N. Altman..1846 to 1847.
Rev. D. Strickler ....1847 to 1851.
Rev. Henry Staub...1851 to 1858.
Rev. S. Vonneida...1859 to 1866.
Rev. Ezekiel Light..1866 to 1869.
Rev. William Mittendorf.............................1869.............

EDITOR OF "WOMAN'S EVANGEL."

Mrs. L. R. Keister, M. A...........................1881.............

SECRETARIES OF THE BOARD OF MISSIONS.

Rev. J. C. Bright..1853 to 1857.
Rev. D. K. Flickinger, D. D..........................1857.............
(Rev. J. C. Bright acted as Secretary for a
number of months during 1857 and 1858, but
was compelled by declining health to leave
the work.)

TREASURERS OF THE BOARD OF MISSIONS.

Rev. John Kemp ....1853 to 1869.
Rev. William McKee.....................................1869 to 1873.
Rev. J. W. Hott ....1873 to 1877.
Rev. J. K. Billheimer....................................1877.............

EDUCATIONAL INSTITUTIONS.

Otterbein University — Westerville, Ohio. Founded, 1847.

Hartsville College — Hartsville, Indiana. Founded, 1852.

Western College — Toledo, Iowa. Founded, 1856.

Lane University — Lecompton, Kansas. Founded, 1865.

Philomath College — Philomath, Oregon. Founded, 1865.

Westfield College — Westfield, Illinois. Founded, 1865.

Lebanon Valley College — Annville, Pennsylvania. Founded, 1867.

Roanoke Academy — Roanoke, Indiana. Founded, 1867.

Avalon College — Avalon, Missouri. Founded, as *Academy,* 1869; as *College,* 1881.

Green Hill Seminary — Green Hill, Indiana. Founded, 1869.

Union Biblical Seminary—Theological—Dayton, Ohio. Founded, 1871.

Edwards Academy — White Pine, Tennessee. Founded, 1877.

Shenandoah Institute — Dayton, Virginia. Founded, 1877.

San Joaquin Valley College — Woodbridge, California. Founded, 1878.

Fostoria Academy — Fostoria, Ohio. Founded, 1879.

Washington Seminary — Huntsville, Washington Territory. Founded, 1880.

Gould College — Harlan, Kansas. Founded, 1881.

Dover Academy — Dover, Illinois. Founded, 1882.

West Virginia Academy — Buckhannon, W. Va. Founded, 1882.

Erie Conference Seminary — Sugar Grove, Warren County, Pa. - Founded, 1884.

Desired information may be obtained from the Presidents and Principals of these institutions.

SPECIAL NOTICE!

Every man, woman and youth of intelligence ought to be a constant reader of good papers and books. Every such person should be a regular and frequent patron of a good book-store and printing-house. "Knowledge is power," and it was the recognition of the value of knowledge, as well as of true religion, which led to the establishment of our denominational Publishing House. To disseminate a pure Christian literature, which shall supplement the work of the preacher and teacher in securing growth in character and knowledge, is its highest aim. But to fulfill its mission, it must have the *hearty support of the people*. The pernicious books and papers now so freely circulated, deserve nothing but contempt. To counteract their influence should be the endeavor of all good people. This can be done by purchasing nothing but good literature.

Our Publishing House issues many excellent publications from its own presses. To most of them attention is called in the following pages, with the hope that in this way our people may be induced to supply themselves with the wholesome intellectual and spiritual food which they contain. They will be sent, post-paid, for the prices annexed. All of our publications should be read by our members.

In addition to the sale of our own publications, we are engaged in the general book-trade, supplying any good book in the market.

For complete list of our own publications, and for catalogues of select books on sale, apply to us by letter. We issue several catalogues, as follows:

1. *Catalogue of Our Own Publications.*
2. *Catalogue of Theological and Religious Books.*
3. *Catalogue of Miscellaneous Books.*
4. *Catalogue of Sunday-school Books and Supplies.*

Rev. W. J. SHUEY,
United Brethren Publishing House,
DAYTON, OHIO.

51

SUNDAY-SCHOOL PERIODICALS.

All Sunday-school workers are requested to examine our line of SUNDAY-SCHOOL PERIODICALS, which embraces a Magazine for Teachers, and Lesson Helps and Papers for scholars of various ages.

OUR BIBLE TEACHER.

A Monthly Teachers' Magazine, containing extensive and valuable comments upon the International Series of Lessons, and, in addition, exercises for the blackboard by Frank Beard, lesson dictionary, map, opening exercises, and miscellaneous editorial and other contributions. It is ably edited, and is issued in handsome style, with good type and first-class paper. Single copy, per annum, 60 cents. *Club Rates:* Five copies or more, to one address, 50 cents per copy per annum. Send for sample.

OUR BIBLE LESSON QUARTERLY.

For advanced scholars. Thirty-two pages. Issued on the first of January, April, July, and October of each year. This Quarterly contains the lessons for three months in a neat cover, and, when space will allow, several pages of original music, prepared expressly for this Quarterly. To make all the lessons available to classes, subscriptions must be sent in before the beginning of the calendar quarters, January 1st, April 1st, July 1st, and October 1st. Not less than five copies should be ordered at one time. Price, 12 cents per copy, per annum; at the same rate for three, six, or nine months.

OUR INTERMEDIATE BIBLE LESSON QUARTERLY.

For intermediate scholars. Issued on the first of January, April, July, and October of each year. Sixteen pages, with a lesson on each page. It has a neat cover, and may be severed by drawing a knife through the back, and be distributed in leaves every two weeks if preferred. No orders for less than 10 copies will be received. Subscriptions must begin on the first of January, April, July, or October. Price, 6 cents per copy, per annum; at the same rate for three, six or nine months. In ordering this Quarterly the word *Intermediate* must be given.

SUNDAY - SCHOOL PERIODICALS.

CHILDREN'S FRIEND and MISSION-ARY VISITOR.

Both Sunday-school papers are each published twice a month —*The Children's Friend* being dated on the first and fifteenth, and *The Missionary Visitor* on the eighth and twenty-second, of each month. These two papers are designed to supply schools with papers for four Sabbaths every month, a want felt in most Sabbath-schools. The price for single copies, per annum, is 30 cents. In clubs, 24 cents per copy per annum.

LESSONS FOR THE LITTLE ONES.

A new and beautifully illustrated paper, adapted to the wants of children from one year old to ten. The paper contains four small pages, printed on new type, and a number is issued for every Sabbath in the year. Each number contains a simple statement of the Sunday-school lesson for the week for which it is issued. Price, in clubs, 20 cents per copy per annum.

THE JUGEND PILGER.

A semi-monthly German Sabbath-school paper; same size as *The Children's Friend.* Terms, for single copies or in clubs, same as *Children's Friend* and *Missionary Visitor.*

All of the above publications are carefully edited, with the view of obtaining the best results in the Christian training of the young. Unsectarian in character, they are adapted to the wants of all Sunday-schools; but as they are prepared by our own Church, and are equal to any and superior to many similar publications, they deserve the full patronage of our own people, and should *unhesitatingly* be used in *every United Brethren* Sabbath-school. Sample copies of all these publications will be promptly forwarded to any address upon application. Address,

W. J. SHUEY, Publisher,
UNITED BRETHREN PUBLISHING HOUSE,
DAYTON, O.

THE LIFE OF

Rev. Philip William Otterbein,

FOUNDER OF THE CHURCH OF THE

United Brethren in Christ.

BY

REV. A. W. DRURY, A. M.,

Professor of Church-History in Union Biblical Seminary.

With an introduction by

BISHOP J. WEAVER, D. D.

The United Brethren Church has waited long for this book. This valuable account of the life of the great Otterbein, the founder of our church, should be read by *every member* of the denomination. The author has discovered many facts of great historic interest never before presented to the public, and has produced a biography which has elicited the highest commendation.

"It is saying much, but it is the truth, that you have done justice to the subject of your book. No one will come after you with a Life of Otterbein. I think you have found all the material extant, and have put it in excellent shape. It is a live book, and the editions should succeed each other rapidly. The publishers, too, have done their work handsomely."— *John Lawrence,* author of U. B. Church History.

"This is a very valuable work. Prof. Drury has studied his subject with extraordinary care, and has produced a volume which is not only creditable to its author, but to the religious denomination which he represents."—*Rev. J. H. Dubbs, D. D.,. in The Guardian.*

"The man of whose life this book is a record, has been largely influential in the religious history of modern times."' —*Western Christian Advocate, Cincinnati.*

The book contains 384 pages, with Steel Plate Portraits of Otterbein and Martin Boehm, and fine illustrations of Otterbein's Church in Baltimore, present parsonage in Baltimore,. Dillenburg in the eighteenth century, and Isaac Long's house and barn, and many other pleasing attractions. No more acceptable present could be made to your minister or friends. The book is printed on fine toned paper, elegantly bound in cloth and gold, and makes an admirable volume. Price, only $1.20, post-paid. Address,

REV. W. J. SHUEY, Dayton, Ohio.

HISTORY OF THE CHURCH

OF THE

UNITED BRETHREN IN CHRIST.

BY

JOHN LAWRENCE.

———

For all who desire an extended account of the United Brethren Church, this volume will be most appropriate. It embraces the history of the Church from its origin to 1861. The information given is full, and the style entertaining. While a number of books of more recent date may give more complete and reliable information concerning particular men, periods, and departments of the Church, this work must remain, for some time to come, the standard general history of the denomination. It is printed from large and clear type, two volumes in one, of 847 pages, and is substantially bound in sheep. 8vo. Price, $2.50. Address,

Rev. W. J. SHUEY,
Dayton, Ohio.

LIFE OF

REV. DAVID EDWARDS, D. D.,

Formerly a Bishop of the Church of the

UNITED BRETHREN IN CHRIST.

BY

Rev. Lewis Davis, D. D.,

With an Introduction by Rev. J. W. Hott, D. D.

———

A faithful history of a long and useful life. Every family in the United Brethren Church should have a copy. 322 pages, 12mo., cloth, with steel likeness of Bishop Edwards. Price, only $1.00, post-paid to any address. Send orders to

REV. W. J. SHUEY,
Dayton, Ohio.

BOOKS ON MISSION-WORK.

THE CHURCH'S MARCHING ORDERS; or, Suggestive Thoughts on the Missionary Work. By Rev. D. K. Flickinger, D. D. 132 pages. 12mo, cloth.. 60

ETHIOPIA; or, Twenty Years of Missionary Life in Western Africa. By Rev. D. K. Flickinger, D. D. 12mo., cloth..................... 1 00

HISTORY OF SHERBRO MISSION, WEST AFRICA. Under the direction of the Missionary Society of the United Brethren in Christ. By Rev. W. McKee. 16mo., cloth..................... 75

ITINERANT SYSTEM AS A MEANS OF GOSPEL EVANGELIZATION, THE. By Rev. J. V. Potts. 92 pages, 18mo., cloth.................... 35

MINISTERIAL SALARY. An exhaustive discussion on the subject of Ministerial Support. A much-needed work among our people. By Bishop J. Weaver, D. D. 16mo., cloth... 30

DISCIPLINE OF THE CHURCH OF THE UNITED BRETHREN IN CHRIST. This is the official Book of Discipline of the Church. In addition to a brief account of the origin of the denomination, it contains its Confession of Faith, its Constitution, its Formulas, and its Rules of Government. An intimate acquaintance with its provisions is important both for preachers and people. English, 24mo., cloth.. 30
German, 24mo., cloth.................................. 30

Address,

Rev. W. J. SHUEY,

DAYTON, OHIO.

JOURNEYINGS

IN THE

OLD WORLD

BY

J. W. HOTT, D. D.

SOLD BY SUBSCRIPTION ONLY.

ACTIVE AGENTS

Wanted in every County, City, and Town in the
United States.

FIRST-CLASS TERMS OFFERED.

For further particulars address,

W. J. SHUEY, PUBLISHER,

DAYTON, OHIO.

HYMNS FOR THE SANCTUARY AND SOCIAL WORSHIP.

WITH TUNES.

No. 1. Cloth sides, leather back, with red edges and side-stamp $1 35
No. 2. Colored Leather, red edges and gilt side-stamp.... 1 75
No. 3. Morocco, gilt edges and gilt side-stamp.................. 2 50
No. 4. Levant Morocco, cushion bevel, antique, full gilt.. 4 00
No. 5. Levant Morocco, Divinity Circuit, flexible, gilt edges.. 5 00

WORDS ONLY. 18mo.

No. 1. Roan, embossed.. 75
No. 2. Roan, embossed, gilt edges.................................... 1 00
No. 3. Imitation Morocco, extra gilt................................ 1 25
No. 4. Imitation Morocco, extra gilt, clasp..................... 1 50
No. 5. Turkey Morocco, extra gilt.................................... 1 75

HYMN BOOKS—German.
No. 1. Colored Leather, embossed.................................... 1 00
No. 2. Morocco, gilt.. 1 35

HARPS—English.
No. 1. Plain Sheep.. 35

HARFENTOENE—German.
No. 1. Roan... 30

SONGSTERS—English.
Christian Songster. Plain Sheep..................................... 45

MISCELLANEOUS BOOKS.

AGE WE LIVE IN, The. Its Dangers and Duties. With a Topical and Chronological Analysis of the Book of Revelation. In three parts: Part I.—The Vials. Part II.—The Age of Errors. Part III.—Danger and Duty of the Church. By Jacob Hoke.............................$1 20

AN APPEAL TO MATTER OF FACT AND COMMON
Sense; or, A Rational Demonstration of Man's Cor-
rupt and Lost Estate. By J. Fletcher. New and
revised edition, with an Introduction by Bishop D.
Edwards, D. D. 50

AUTOBIOGRAPHY OF REV. LYDIA SEXTON. 655
pages. Crown 8vo., cloth, with steel portrait of the
author. 2 00

CLUSTERS FROM ESHCOL; or, Words of Comfort and
Encouragement drawn from the Sacred Scriptures for
the Afflicted Children of God. By Jacob Hoke. 357
pages, 12mo., cloth. 1 00

DISCOURSES ON THE RESURRECTION. By Bishop
Jonathan Weaver, D. D. 60

DIVINE PROVIDENCE. History of the Doctrine; Its
Nature and Reasonableness; Providence—Particular,
General, and Universal; Controlling Good and Evil;
Mysterious; Consolation Derived from a Belief in the
Doctrine of Divine Providence; Necessity, Import-
ance, and Encouragements to submit to the Providence
of God. By Bishop Jonathan Weaver, D. D. 323 pages,
12mo., cloth. 1 25

DOCTRINE OF UNIVERSAL RESTORATION CARE-
fully Examined, The. By Bishop J. Weaver, D. D.
With steel portrait of the author. 402 pages, 12mo.,
cloth. 1 25

HOLINESS; or, The Higher Christian Life. By Jacob
Hoke. Revised and enlarged edition. 305 pages,
12mo., cloth. 75

LECTURES TO YOUNG MEN ON THE FORMATION
of Character, etc. Originally addressed to the Young
Men of Hartford and New Haven, and published at
their urgent request. By Rev. Joel Hawes, D. D. With
an Introduction by John McCoy. 35

LIGHT ON FREEMASONRY. Revised edition. With
an Appendix Revealing the Mysteries of Odd Fellowship, including Encampment Degrees. By a member
of the Craft. 12mo., cloth. 1 50

Books for the Sabbath-School Library and Home Reading.

THE PIONEER LIBRARY.

1. Little Gate.	6. Is the Bible True?
2. Safe Home.	7. Counsels to Young Men.
3. Little Mary.	8. City Cousins.
4. Men of Worth.	9. Guiding Star.
5. May Earnest.	10. Introduction to Bible Study.

These books are of permanent value, adapted to all ages of youth, and tastefully bound in cloth. Price per set of 10 volumes.. 5 00

BRICKEY SORREL; or, The Twin Cousins. By Mrs. Isadore S. Bash. 254 pages. The book narrates the upward progress of its leading character, from poverty and obscurity to a most honorable place as a minister of the gospel. The real object of the volume is to present in strong pictures the desolating power of intemperance. This feature is wrought out in the sad history of the lives of other characters in the story. The book is written in fascinating style, and will be read with great interest and profit.................... 75

MY FIVE WARDS; or, Aunt Huldah's Homilies. 236 pages. By Mrs. Julia McNair Wright. This volume is replete with practical thoughts on practical subjects, of especial value to young ladies and girls approaching young ladyhood. The sage counsels of Aunt Huldah are presented in the form of conversation, strung—as the author aptly expresses it—on the merest thread of story. Common sense of rare soundness and a deep reverence for Bible authority, characterize the book.. 75

THE GOSPEL IN THE RIVIERA. A Story of Italy. By Mrs. Julia McNair Wright. 224 pp. The popular author of this book has given us in its pages one of the choicest productions of her fruitful pen. The book details the struggles and sufferings of the Waldensian Protestants in their conflicts with Romanism. The facts on which it is founded were gathered by the author during her residence in Italy, and are presented with a vividness possible only to one who has been on the ground where the scenes are laid......................... 75

THE VINES OF ESHCOL. By Rev. J. B. Robinson. 133 pages. The book is full of valuable thought for workers in Christ's vineyard. The author, a president of a New England College, is a man of scholarly habits, and a close thinker. In style, the book combines in happy proportions, beauty of ornament, and sterling solidity. Will be most valuable for young or older readers.. 50

SUNDAY-SCHOOL SUPPLIES.

We desire to call the attention of all Sunday-school workers to our facilities for supplying all wants of Sunday-schools at reasonable prices. In addition to our line of periodicals, our stock embraces:

Sunday-School Libraries.

We carry an immense stock of Sunday-school library books, comprising not only books in complete sets, put up in boxes, but also select and miscellaneous books in various departments of literature, adapted to all ages and tastes. These books are offered at the most favorable terms.

Books on Organizing and Conducting Sunday-schools;
Blank Minute, Record, and Class Books;
Bibles and Testaments;
Helps for Superintendents and Teachers;
Sabbath-school Music Books;
Sabbath-school Tickets and Cards;
Blackboards and Maps;
Chautauqua Normal Outline and Text-books;
Anything else you may need.

For the convenience of our customers, we have prepared a CATALOGUE of our Sunday-school Supplies, which we will send free of charge to any address. Correspondence is solicited.

Address,

Rev. W. J. SHUEY,
DAYTON, OHIO.

POPULAR SUNDAY-SCHOOL MUSIC BOOKS.

The attention of all Sunday-school workers is called to the following choice SUNDAY-SCHOOL MUSIC BOOKS, of which hundreds of thousands have been sold:

HOLY VOICES.

Our latest Sunday-school music book. By Revs. E. S. Lorenz and Isaiah Baltzell. Fresh, and equal, if not superior, to anything yet produced for Sunday-schools. 192 pages, board cover.

SONGS OF THE KINGDOM.

A choice selection of Sunday-school Gems from *Gates of Praise, Heavenly Carols, Golden Songs,* and *Songs of the Cross,* by Revs. I. Baltzell and E. S. Lorenz, with complete Course of Instruction in Musical Notation. 208 pages, board cover.

GATES OF PRAISE.

By Revs. I. Baltzell and E. S. Lorenz. One of the latest and best Sunday-school singing books, containing songs for every occasion of interest. Suitable, also, for praise and prayer-meetings. 192 pages, board cover.

HEAVENLY CAROLS.

By Revs. I. Baltzell and E. S. Lorenz, assisted by Prof. J. H. Kurzenknabe and Rev. A. A. Graley. The best hymnal and musical talent in the land has been drawn upon to furnish materials for the above book. The music will be found simple and easy. The book contains a New and Improved Elementary Department. 176 pages, board cover.

GOLDEN SONGS.

By Rev. Isaiah Baltzell. One of the most popular Sunday-school music books ever published. Including an Elementary and Practical Department on the Theory of Music, by Prof. J. H. Kurzenknabe, which has been tried and approved by hundreds of music teachers. 176 pages, board cover.

SONGS OF THE CROSS.

By Rev. E. S. Lorenz. Over fifty contributors have aided in making Songs of the Cross. It contains an Elementary Department teaching how to read music. 160 pages, board cover.

PILGER LIEDER.

This is the title of a German Hymn and Tune Book for Sunday-schools. It contains 238 Hymns, of which 180 are set to music. 191 pages, board cover. Price, 35 cents per single copy, or 30 cents when ordered by the dozen copies, post-paid; $3.00 per dozen by express, express charges unpaid.

SONGS OF GRACE.

Designed for revival meetings, camp-meetings, prayer and praise-meetings, and for the sanctuary and home. By Revs. I. Baltzell and E. S. Lorenz. Single copy, 25 cents. Per hundred, $20.00. Per dozen by express, $2.50; by mail, $3.00.

THE PRICES of *Holy Voices, Songs of the Kingdom, Gates of Praise, Heavenly Carols, Golden Songs,* and *Songs of the Cross* are as follows: 35 cents per single copy by mail; $4.00 per dozen by mail, post-paid; $3.60 per dozen by express, express charges unpaid; $30.00 per hundred by express. The prices of *Pilger Lieder* and *Songs of Grace* are mentioned above under their respective titles. Of any of the above books, SPECIMEN PAGES FREE.

Rev. W. J. SHUEY, Publisher,
DAYTON, OHIO.

United Brethren
Home Reading Circle.

—◦◦┊●┊◦◦—

I. INTRODUCTORY.

The United Brethren Sabbath-school Board, believing that a large and ever-increasing number of the people of our Church, and others about them, both young and old, may be induced to enter upon and pursue a course of reading and study at home that will introduce them to new fields of inquiry and knowledge, and to avenues of usefulness, honor, and profit not before thought of; and believing further that organization, general and local, will aid greatly in attaining the objects indicated, proposes to the Church the *plan of organization* herewith given, with the belief and hope that its general approval and adoption will lead to eminently beneficial results. The preliminary steps for forming this organization were taken at the semi-annual meeting of the Board on the 27th of October, 1880, at Westerville, Ohio, and the plan as now offered was perfected at a meeting held in Dayton, Ohio, December 18th, 1880.

———

II. PLAN OF ORGANIZATION.

THE HOME READING-CIRCLE OF THE UNITED BRETHREN IN CHRIST.

1. This organization shall be under the auspices and direction of the general Sabbath-school Board of the Church.
2. Its aim shall be to promote home-reading and culture in a systematic and progressive manner.
3. The supervision and promotion of this study shall belong primarily to local circles, and shall end with graduation under the officers of the Sabbath-school Board.
4. The full course of study shall embrace three years, and shall consist of biblical, historical, scientific, and literary branches.
5. Persons desiring to become members of the Home Reading-Circle shall forward their names, with statement of age,

68

whether married or single, and church-membership, to the General Secretary of the Sabbath-school Board [Robert Cowden, Galion, Ohio].

6. Members constituting a local circle shall be diligent in study, devoting a fair average proportion of each week-day to the studies in hand.

7. Members shall pay an annual fee of fifty cents, for the purpose of defraying the expenses of the organization, such as correspondence, printing, etc. The money shall be forwarded to the corresponding secretary at the time of joining, and on the first of each January thereafter. It may be sent by draft, money order, postal note, or in fractional currency or two-cent postage stamps, at the risk of the sender.

8. Local circles may hold meetings weekly, semi-monthly, or as often as practicable, and organize with the usual officers, for the promotion of the studies in course, with such extra lectures, discussions, essays, and drills, as may seem profitable. Any one may belong to the organization, even where local circles can not be formed. But, wherever possible, circles should be formed and sustained with energy.

9. The annual examination shall be conducted by the officers of the Sabbath-school Board, at their annual meeting in the spring, upon written replies to questions, sent to the secretary as early as April 1st.

10. The organization may be entered at the beginning of any calendar year, in the manner before stated.

11. At the completion of the full course of reading a diploma will be given to the graduate.

III. ENDORSEMENT.

Since the organization of the Circle the General Conference held at Lisbon, Iowa, put upon the enterprise the *unanimous* seal of its approbation in the following language:

"V. We heartily approve of the action of the Sunday-school Board in projecting and organizing the United Brethren Home Reading-Circle; and, believing that its general acceptance by our people will tend greatly to the promotion of intelligence and the best forms of culture among them, we would *earnestly advise and encourage the promotion of reading-circles wherever it may be found practicable.*"

IV. READING.

The books to be read in 1885 are as follows:

January—Life of Otterbein. Drury - - - - $1 00
February—The Christian Sabbath. Dabney - - - 45
    Hand-Book of the United Brethren in Christ,
     Flexible Leather - - - 35 cents.
     Flexible Cloth - - - 15 cents.
     Manilla - - - - - - - 10

V. SUGGESTIONS.

It is expected that each member will read an average of forty minutes each week-day, and that in the summer months the study will be lighter and in winter heavier. Also, that during the season usually devoted to revival-meetings the reading will, as far as possible, conduce to that end.

There is every encouragement to begin at once. The reading for 1885 will be less arduous and expensive than that of some of the former years. We begin the year with the new and invaluable book by Prof. Drury, of Union Biblical Seminary, entitled the LIFE OF OTTERBEIN, just from our own press, and the high standard of the reading is well sustained throughout the year.

For a full and explicit statement of similarity and of differences between the Home Reading Circle and the Chautauqua Literary and Scientific Circle, and between both of those and the Sunday-school Normal Course, now changed to the Assembly Normal Union, see the writer's article on the first page of the *Religious Telescope*, for January 2, 1884. Many people get these different institutions confounded in their minds.

Many very valuable testimonials of approval and high appreciation have come to the secretary from those reading in the course, for which there is no room here.

Without extending these remarks further, it is hoped that the reader will use his influence to secure the offered advantages to his field of labor or circle of acquaintances, aiding in the formation of circles, and report at once to me.

Membership in the United Brethren or any other church is not essential to membership in the circle. Its advantages are open and free to all alike.

For books, address Rev. W. J. Shuey, Dayton, Ohio. For the encouragement of all in the circle, all books are marked down to the *lowest possible figures*, and will be sent by mail prepaid for the prices named above.

Correspondence solicited. Circulars sent free on application to

ROBERT COWDEN, Secretary,
GALION, OHIO.

A HAND-BOOK
OF THE
UNITED BRETHREN IN CHRIST.
By PROF. E. L. SHUEY, A. M.,
Of Otterbein University.

A Brief Compen lium of the History, Doctrine, Government, and General Sund.iy-school, Missionary, Publishing, and Educational Work of the United Brethren Church, with Historical Tables of General Church Officers and Educational Institutions.

"It undertakes to give, in condensed form, intelligent answers to the natural inquiries of those who are seeking a good general view of our Church. * * * * The merit of the Hand-Book is, that it brings select materials together in a short, well written, and highly interesting sketch. We hope the service which the author renders will be fully appreciated by our ministers and people, and that, at the very low price at which it is sold, it may reach every nook and corner of the Church."—*Religious Telescope.*

"The little work is really invaluable for the purpose for which it was prepared. Wherever it goes it will make enthusiastic United Brethren. It ought to be vigorously pushed all over the Church. Every family in the Church ought to have a copy. Ministers will serve the interests of the Church, and their own as well, by calling the attention of the people to the little book from the pulpit and in private. Converts and new members especially should be persuaded to purchase and read it. In communities where our Church has just begun to work, the little book ought to be scattered broadcast in and out of the Church. It will often be wise to give away copies of the book where it will do good. If twenty-five or thirty thousand copies of this hand-book could be distributed through the Church during the next three or four years, I am sure its beneficent influence would be felt in every line [of church-work. It will beget intelligent interest in the Church, and prepare the way for more members, more money, and more work."—*E. D. Mund.*

It is an indispensable aid to an intelligent knowledge of our Church. *Every man, woman, and child* in the denomination should read it. *Every minister* should *welcome* it as an *invaluable assistant* in his work. He should speak of it *from the pulpit,* and *personally* see that *every member of his charge* is supplied with it. It is of special interest to *outsiders,* as giving them such a knowledge of this branch of the Church as every Christian should possess. Send for it at once, and introduce it to the people. The price is low. Net prices, post-paid: Manilla cover, cut flush, single copy, 10 cents, per dozen, $1.20; flexible cloth, cut flush, red edges, gilt side-stamp, single copy, 15 cents, per dozen, $1.80; flexible leather, gilt edges and side-stamp, extra paper, single copy, 35 cents, per dozen, $4.20. Address,

REV. W. J. SHUEY,
UNITED BRETHREN PUBLISHING HOUSE,
DAYTON, OHIO.

NEW

SUNDAY - SCHOOL SONG BOOK

FOR 1885.

Notes of Victory.

—BY—

E. S. LORENZ and W. A. OGDEN.

The Completest and Best with which either author has ever
been connected. Easy and Melodious. New and stirring
Sunday - school Songs, Standard Hymns with Tunes, Opening
and Closing Exercises for Special Occasions. Everything is
provided for. 192 pages, good print, good paper, beautiful
cover.

Ready About April 1.

Usual prices. 35 cents per single copy by mail, post-paid;
$4.00 per dozen by mail, post-paid; $3.60 per dozen by express,
express charges unpaid. *Send for Sample.*

Address,

W. J. SHUEY,

UNITED BRETHREN PUBLISHING HOUSE,

DAYTON, OHIO.

www.ingramcontent.com/pod-product-compliance
Lightning Source LLC
Chambersburg PA
CBHW020238090426
42735CB00010B/1753